We Are One

How the World Adds Up

Susan Hood

illustrated by
Linda Yan

CANDLEWICK PRESS

One *can be one thing*
all on its own—
one star,
one stream,
one stick,
one stone.

The idea that the whole is greater than the sum of its parts is often credited to Aristotle, an ancient Greek philosopher.

But those on their toes, those using their smarts,
know one can be more than the sum of its parts.

Just think: Many single sticks add up to one pile of sticks, but they can also be something more, like a bird's nest, a beaver dam, or a campfire. Likewise, many streams flow into a single river, and many stars make up a galaxy. What could many stones make?

One sandwich requires **two** *slices of bread.*

The sandwich got its name in the 1700s from British statesman John Montagu, fourth Earl of Sandwich, who asked for salt beef between two slices of bread. However, the first recorded sandwich was created by Hillel the Elder, a Jewish leader and scholar who lived in the first century BCE.

Two vows make one marriage when friends want to wed.

In 2015, US Supreme Court Justice Anthony Kennedy wrote, "In forming a marital union, two people become something greater than once they were." They become a family.

Three *lines craft a poem that is called a haiku.*

A haiku is a traditional Japanese form of unrhymed poetry, originally written as one vertical line and measured in morae, or breaths. Haiku taught in English usually have three lines and a set structure: five syllables in the first line, seven in the second, and five in the third. Haiku are typically keen observations about single moments in time, usually refer to nature or the natural world, and often allude to season or time of day.

Three *letters together spell out the word you!*

Yellow starlight shines
On ones I'm missing tonight,
Urging me to write.

Letters add up to words. Words add up to sentences. Many stories and poems follow the rule of three, a writing principle that suggests characters and events are more satisfying when they come in threes. Just think of "The Three Little Pigs" and "Three Billy Goats Gruff." From a three-ring circus to the three primary colors, the rule of three (*omne trium perfectum* in Latin) says trios equal perfection.

Four *points on a compass help chart the frontier.*

The needle on a compass always points to the north because the magnet inside is attracted to the earth's magnetic North Pole. (Note that this is different from the geographic North Pole, which is about 1,000 miles farther north.) The compass is celebrated as one of the four great inventions of ancient China—along with gunpowder, papermaking, and printing—that significantly changed the world.

The four seasons of spring, summer, autumn, and winter are caused by the tilt of Earth on its axis as it circles the sun. The weather is warmer in places where the sun's rays hit most directly and cooler in places that are tilted away from the sun.

Five *elegant moves form the core of ballet.*

New dancers begin ballet by learning five basic positions for their feet and arms. They are simply called first position, second position, third position, and so on. The dancers then add three basic movements: plié (plee-AY): bending the knees; relevé (reh-luh-VAY): rising; and sauté (soh-TAY): jumping. After that, they're ready to add arabesques, pirouettes, and grands jetés!

Like most classical plays, all of Shakespeare's plays are divided into five acts. Act 1 introduces the characters, setting, and conflict. Act 2 presents complications in the story. Act 3 builds to a climax or a crossroads. Act 4 reveals the consequences. Act 5 ends the story. Shakespeare didn't divide his plays this way. This was done after his death by Nicholas Rowe, an early editor of Shakespeare's work.

A B C D E F G

H I J K L M N

O P Q R S T U

V W X Y Z

Braille writing uses what's called a Braille cell, a grid of six dots arranged in two columns of three. The dots in each cell are raised in sixty-four different combinations to represent each letter of the alphabet as well as numbers and punctuation marks. People who are blind or have limited vision can read with their fingers by feeling the dots on the page.

Six *sides form a snowflake, an icy lace veil.*

No two snowflakes are alike! Water droplets in a cloud freeze into ice around a speck of dust or pollen in the air. Then other water droplets attach themselves, most often forming six sides as a result of the way water molecules bond. As a snowflake falls, it changes shape when it bumps into other snowflakes and when it hits different temperatures or humidity levels on the way down.

RED
ORANGE
YELLOW
GREEN
BLUE
INDIGO
VIOLET

One rainbow paints skies using **seven** *bright hues.*

NORTH
ATLANTIC
OCEAN

SOUTH
ATLANTIC
OCEAN

ROY-G-BIV is a hint used to remember the seven colors in visible light (the colors humans can see): red, orange, yellow, green, blue, indigo, and violet. Many bees, birds, and fish and even some mammals can see ultraviolet light (colors beyond violet).

ARCTIC
OCEAN

NORTH
PACIFIC
OCEAN

INDIAN
OCEAN

SOUTH
PACIFIC
OCEAN

SOUTHERN
OCEAN

The term "seven seas" comes from ancient Mesopotamia and referred to the bodies of water known at the time. The list changed as explorers sailed farther afield. The modern-day seven are the Arctic, North Atlantic, South Atlantic, Indian, North Pacific, South Pacific, and Southern Oceans, the seas that circle the seven continents on the globe.

*Once old Spanish dollars were pieces of **eight**.*

Early American colonists used whatever foreign coins were at hand for currency. The most common was the Spanish silver dollar (worth eight Spanish reales), legal tender in America until 1857. To make change, people cut the coin into eighths, creating the "pieces of eight" celebrated in pirate lore.

Eight *sides make a shape meaning, please stop and wait!*

STOP

Eight sides make a shape called an octagon, which is used in many countries for stop signs. So even if you don't know the language on the sign, the shape will tell you what to do.

*In baseball, one team fields **nine** folks to play.*

The nine baseball positions are pitcher, catcher, first baseman, second baseman, third baseman, shortstop, left fielder, center fielder, and right fielder.

Then after **nine** *innings, one team wins the day!*

A baseball measures about nine inches around. And there are nine innings in a professional baseball game (unless the score is tied, in which case, innings are added until the tie is broken).

Ten *years fly by fast and one decade is done.*

Many number systems around the world use a base of ten.

Ten *decades add up to one century's run.*

Ten years make one decade; ten decades, one century; ten centuries, one millennium. It seems a safe bet that humans count by tens because we first learned to count on our ten fingers.

You needn't look far to see that it's true—
this simple equation applies to you, too.
You are one person
but also one part
of a family,
a team,
the world's beating heart.

We're moondust and star shine
all circling the sun.
We're a vast constellation,
and yes . . .

Everything and everyone on Earth is made of tiny particles called atoms. That includes you! Humans share many of the same atoms found in the stars—the elements of hydrogen, carbon, nitrogen, oxygen, sulfur, and phosphorus.

Scientists call these six elements the building blocks of life. They fell to Earth from stars that exploded billions of years ago and continue to do so today. They make their way into plants, the air, and our bodies. As astronomer Carl Sagan once said, "We are made of star-stuff."

Source Notes

"In forming a marital union . . . once they were": Obergefell v. Hodges, 576 U.S. ____ (2015).

"We are made of star-stuff": Carl Sagan, *Carl Sagan's Cosmic Connection*, Cambridge: Cambridge University Press, 2000, 190.

Sources and Resources

The whole is greater than the sum of its parts.
https://plato.stanford.edu/entries/aristotle-metaphysics/#ActuPote
https://www.biography.com/scholar/aristotle

Two slices of bread build one sandwich.
http://www.pbs.org/food/the-history-kitchen/history-sandwich/
https://www.hillel.org/about/news-views/news-views---blog/news-and-views/2015/04/02
    /better-together-hillels-sandwich

Two vows make one marriage.
https://supreme.justia.com/cases/federal/us/576/14-556/opinion3.html

Three lines in a haiku
https://www.poetryfoundation.org/learn/glossary-terms/haiku-or-hokku
https://www.poets.org/poetsorg/text/haiku-poetic-form

The rule of three
https://rule-of-three.co.uk/what-is-the-rule-of-three-copywriting/
https://www.forbes.com/sites/carminegallo/2012/07/02
    /thomas-jefferson-steve-jobs-and-the-rule-of-3/#255a2eb61962

Four cardinal directions on a compass
https://www.scientificamerican.com/article/steering-science-make-a-homemade-compass/
https://www.nationalgeographic.org/encyclopedia/compass/
http://www.fmprc.gov.cn/ce/ceza/eng/zt/zgabc/t165406.htm

Four seasons in an Earth year
https://www.calacademy.org/educators/why-do-we-have-different-seasons

Five fundamental positions in ballet
https://ballethub.com/ballet-lesson/five-basic-positions-ballet/
https://www.abt.org/explore/learn/ballet-dictionary/

Five acts in a Shakespeare play
https://www.folger.edu/shakespeare-unlimited/editing-shakespeare
https://www.storyboardthat.com/articles/e/five-act-structure

Six dots form the basis of Braille.
http://www.afb.org/info/living-with-vision-loss/braille/what-is-braille/123
https://brailleworks.com/braille-resources/history-of-braille/

Six sides on a snowflake
https://www.noaa.gov/stories/how-do-snowflakes-form-science-behind-snow

The Seven Seas
https://oceanservice.noaa.gov/facts/sevenseas.html

Pieces of eight
http://www.exploresrs.org/blog/entry/5

Eight sides to a stop sign
https://www.pbase.com/bmcmorrow/stopsigns

Nine positions on a baseball team
https://www.baseball-reference.com/bullpen/Positions

Nine innings in a baseball game
http://mlb.mlb.com/documents/0/4/0/224919040/2017_Official_Baseball_Rules_dbt69t59.pdf

Base ten
https://www.britannica.com/science/numeral
https://www.thoughtco.com/definition-of-base-10-2312365

Moondust and star shine
https://www.cnet.com/news/we-are-made-of-star-stuff-a-quick-lesson-on-how/
https://www.theguardian.com/science/2017/jul/27/we-are-all-made-of-stars-half-our-bodies-atoms
    -formed-beyond-the-milky-way

Especially for Kids

"Who Was Hillel?"
https://www.myjewishlearning.com/article/hillel/

"How to Write a Haiku" by Kenn Nesbitt, former Children's Poet Laureate
https://www.poetry4kids.com/lessons/how-to-write-a-haiku/

"The Number Three: Number Songs by Storybots"
https://www.youtube.com/watch?v=sppcp-alo_Y

"How Does a Compass Work?"
https://www.wonderopolis.org/wonder/how-does-a-compass-work

"What Causes the Seasons?"
https://spaceplace.nasa.gov/seasons/en/

Firebird by Misty Copeland, illustrated by Christopher Myers. New York: Putnam, 2014.

"Shakespeare for Kids"
https://www.folger.edu/shakespeare-kids

"Who Invented the Braille System?"
https://www.kidsdiscover.com/quick-reads/who-invented-the-braille-system/

"It's Snowing! Fun with Crystals"
https://www.kidsdiscover.com/teacherresources/fun-with-crystals/

"Ocean Facts!"
https://www.natgeokids.com/uk/discover/geography/general-geography/ocean-facts

"Sea History for Kids"
https://seahistory.org/sea-history-for-kids/pieces-of-eight/

"Stop Sign Facts for Kids"
https://kids.kiddle.co/Stop_sign

"Baseball Facts for Kids"
https://kids.kiddle.co/Baseball

"Number and Operations in Base Ten"
https://cptv.pbslearningmedia.org/subjects/mathematics/k-8-mathematics
    /number--operations-in-base-ten/

"Star Stuff: The Story of Carl Sagan" (short film about Sagan as a boy)
https://www.youtube.com/watch?v=PPTnuUcUVVY

More About How the World Adds Up

Here are some other things that come in groups of:

Ten
★ pins in bowling
★ cents in a dime
★ dimes in a dollar
★ legs on a crab
★ legs on a shrimp
★ limbs on a squid
★ numerals in a US phone number
★ types of clouds: stratus, cirrus, cumulus, stratocumulus, cirrostratus, cirrocumulus, nimbostratus, altostratus, altocumulus, and cumulonimbus
★ sides on a decagon

Nine
★ US Supreme Court justices
★ squares in a tic-tac-toe grid
★ months in an average human pregnancy
★ mythical lives for a cat
★ Greek Muses: Calliope, Clio, Erato, Euterpe, Melpomene, Polyhymnia, Terpsichore, Thalia, and Urania
★ Beethoven symphonies
★ twists in the river Styx of Greek mythology
★ sides on a nonagon or enneagon

Eight
★ limbs on an octopus
★ legs on a spider
★ whole notes in an octave
★ reindeer pulling Santa's sleigh: Dasher, Dancer, Prancer, Vixen, Comet, Cupid, Donder, and Blitzen
★ phases of the moon
★ fluid ounces in a cup
★ pints in a gallon
★ sides on an octagon

Seven
★ days in a week
★ dwarfs in the Disney version of *Snow White*: Bashful, Doc, Dopey, Grumpy, Happy, Sleepy, and Sneezy
★ wonders of the ancient world: the Pyramids of Giza, the Hanging Gardens of Babylon, the Statue of Zeus at Olympia, the Temple of Artemis at Ephesus, the Mausoleum at Halicarnassus, the Colossus of Rhodes, and the Lighthouse of Alexandria
★ hills of Rome: Aventine, Caelian, Capitoline, Esquiline, Palatine, Quirinal, and Viminal
★ sides on a heptagon

Six

★ strings on a standard acoustic guitar
★ sides on a cube
★ sides on a beehive cell
★ legs on an insect
★ sides on a hexagon

Five

★ American Great Lakes: Huron, Ontario, Michigan, Erie, and Superior
★ rings in the symbol for the Olympics
★ arms on a sea star
★ points on a star shape
★ W questions: who, what, when, where, and why
★ sides on a pentagon

Four

★ wheels on a car
★ leaves on a lucky clover
★ legs on a chair
★ suits in a deck of playing cards: clubs, diamonds, hearts, and spades
★ members of the band the Beatles: John Lennon, Paul McCartney, George Harrison, and Ringo Starr
★ members in a musical quartet
★ kids in a set of quadruplets
★ natural elements: earth, air, fire, and water
★ basic mathematical operations: addition, subtraction, multiplication, and division
★ sides on a square
★ sides on a rectangle

Three

★ primary colors: red, blue, and yellow
★ secondary colors: purple, orange, and green
★ snowballs in a classic snowman
★ feet in a yard
★ sides on a yield sign
★ teaspoons in a tablespoon
★ hands on a clock: hour, minute, and second
★ legs on an easel
★ original musketeers from the book by Alexandre Dumas: Athos, Porthos, and Aramis
★ wheels on a tricycle
★ wishes in a genie's magical lamp
★ meals a day: breakfast, lunch, and dinner
★ branches of US government: executive, legislative, and judicial

★ strikes and you're out in baseball
★ outs per team in a baseball inning
★ kids in a set of triplets
★ members in a musical trio
★ sides on a triangle

Two

★ in a pair (socks, skates, gloves, mittens, shoes, crutches, cuff links, etc.)
★ blades on a pair of scissors
★ chopsticks to eat with
★ wheels on a bicycle
★ directions in a two-way street
★ bookends
★ wings on a bird
★ earbuds
★ kids in a set of twins
★ lenses in glasses or sunglasses
★ in a set of opposites
★ numerals in a binary number system (0 and 1)
★ sides to a coin

One

★ partridge in a pear tree (from the carol "The Twelve Days of Christmas")
★ performer in a solo
★ dot in a small i
★ direction on a one-way street
★ nose on your face
★ belly button on your stomach
★ golden rule: treat others as you would want to be treated
★ ring to rule them all (from The Lord of the Rings by J. R. R. Tolkien)
★ equator belting Earth
★ Earth
★ **and only one YOU!**

With love for all of the one-of-a-kind
individuals in my one-and-only family
SH

To George and Lisa,
thank you for loving me
LY

Text copyright © 2021 by Susan Hood
Illustrations copyright © 2021 by Linda Yan

First edition 2021

Library of Congress Catalog Card Number pending
ISBN 978-1-5362-0114-7

21 22 23 24 25 26 LEO 10 9 8 7 6 5 4 3 2 1

Printed in Heshan, Guangdong, China

This book was typeset in Gill Sans and Mrs Eaves.
The illustrations were created digitally.

Candlewick Press
99 Dover Street
Somerville, Massachusetts 02144

www.candlewick.com